# 26.2

THINGS TO DO INSTEAD OF
RUNNING A MARATHON

**Jennifer McCartney** is the *New York Times* bestselling author of more than a dozen books, which have been translated into more than 25 languages. She has written about utopias, time machines and train travel for outlets like BBC Radio 4, *The Atlantic*, *Architectural Digest*, *Vice Magazine*, *Teen Vogue* and CBC. Originally from Hamilton, Ontario, she has lived in four countries and held 27 jobs, including at a ski resort, an amusement park and on an island in the Great Lakes. She has degrees from the University of Guelph and the University of Glasgow. She currently lives in Brooklyn, New York.

JENNIFER McCARTNEY

# 26.2

## THINGS TO DO INSTEAD OF RUNNING A MARATHON

LITERALLY ANYTHING ELSE

HODDER & STOUGHTON

First published in Great Britain in 2026 by
Hodder & Stoughton Limited
An Hachette UK company

The authorised representative in the EEA is
Hachette Ireland, 8 Castlecourt Centre, Dublin 15,
D15 XTP3, Ireland (email: info@hbgi.ie)

1

Copyright © Jennifer McCartney 2026

The right of Jennifer McCartney to be identified as the
Author of the Work has been asserted by her in accordance
with the Copyright, Designs and Patents Act 1988.

All rights reserved. No part of this publication may be reproduced,
stored in a retrieval system, or transmitted, in any form or by
any means without the prior written permission of the publisher,
nor be otherwise circulated in any form of binding or cover
other than that in which it is published and without a similar
condition being imposed on the subsequent purchaser.

Illustrations by Joanna Boyle © Hodder & Stoughton 2026

A CIP catalogue record for this title is
available from the British Library

Hardback ISBN 9781399756914
ebook ISBN 9781399756921

Typeset in PSFournier by Hewer Text UK Ltd, Edinburgh
Printed and bound in Great Britain by Clays Ltd, Elcograf S.p.A.

Hodder & Stoughton policy is to use papers that are natural, renewable
and recyclable products and made from wood grown in sustainable
forests. The logging and manufacturing processes are expected to
conform to the environmental regulations of the country of origin.

Hodder & Stoughton Limited
Carmelite House
50 Victoria Embankment
London EC4Y 0DZ

www.hodder.co.uk

'How do you know if someone ran a marathon? Don't worry, they'll tell you.'

JIMMY FALLON

# Contents

Introduction — 1

1. Plant Something — 4
2. Learn to Bartend and Host a Fancy Cocktail Party — 8
3. Plan Your Funeral — 12
4. Take Up Watercolours — 16
5. Go Fish (Learn a Card Game) — 20
6. Go Wild Swimming — 24
7. Adopt a Rescue Animal (Goose or Snake) — 28
8. Refurbish an Old Bit of Furniture — 32
9. Learn Five Phrases in a New Language — 36
10. Explore Some Cookie Recipes — 40
11. Become an Amateur Astronomer — 44
12. Mend Your Own Clothing — 48
13. Knit Something — 52
14. Become a Beachcomber — 56
15. Embrace the Supernatural — 60
16. Take Dancing Lessons — 64

| | | |
|---|---|---|
| 17. | Write a Poem | 68 |
| 18. | Make Your Own Jam | 72 |
| 19. | Take a Pottery Course | 76 |
| 20. | Master a Magic Trick | 80 |
| 21. | Become Known for Sending Handwritten Letters | 84 |
| 22. | Learn to Identify Seven Birds | 88 |
| 23. | Start a Compost Heap | 92 |
| 24. | Write to Your MP | 96 |
| 25. | Train for a Long-Distance Walk (Slowly) | 100 |
| 26. | Learn to Change a Tyre | 104 |
| 26.2 | Watch a Marathon | 108 |

| | |
|---|---|
| The Finish Line | 111 |
| Acknowledgements | 113 |

# Introduction

'The marathon always starts after 30km. That's where the problems start. You start without any problems, without any pain. All the pain comes after 30km. Sometimes, it's possible to have pain even in the finger.'*

**Haile Gebrselassie**

Marathon running is big business. Around 1.1 million people finish one annually. (That's about 0.01% of the world's population.) In New York City, Chicago, London, Tokyo, Toronto and Boston, every year, members of this elite group participate in uplifting, healthy, community-focused love fests that bring out the best in everyone. Sportsmanship!

*If this sounds like fun, this isn't the book for you. Enjoy your finger pain and eventual knee replacement.

Team spirit! Fitness! There's a kind of moral goodness associated with the whole endeavour.

Why? Running a marathon signifies to the world that you've put in the work, the training and the hours to better yourself. Completing one is a status symbol, of sorts. It affords the runner a bit of cultural cachet. It's early mornings and lean protein lunches. What self-discipline! Bravo, you. Make sure to post an endorphin-fuelled self-congratulatory photo online once you're done.

But the fact is, more than 99% of us across the globe have better things to do with our time. We are the late risers, the night owls, the boozers, the genetically disinclined, the strollers and amblers, the ones who'd rather not rush. We're the 'smell the roses' types. The 'let's watch one more episode' and 'let's stay in, it's raining' types.

This is the book for us. And if you've got a recovering marathon runner in your life, it's a great gift for them, too.

## 26.2 THINGS TO DO INSTEAD OF RUNNING A MARATHON

Packed within these pages are myriad fun, silly and engaging options of things to do *instead* of running a marathon. None of these will impact your ankles or knees. And all of them are entertaining. The opposite of running, probably. I wouldn't know.* This light-hearted manual offers a host of fun suggestions along with step-by-step instructions for making the most of your luxurious, sedentary ways.

Get ready to bake, beach, bartend, brunch and generally live life like the amazing, chill, Type B person you are.

---

*When I was 13, our PE teacher made us run one kilometre through the woods and I vomited afterwards.

# Plant Something

'An addiction to gardening is
not all bad when you consider
all the other choices in life.'

**Cora Lea Bell**

This may sound twee but the fact is that planting, gardening and generally being among growing living things is a fantastic way to spend your time on this planet. Gardening can also improve your mental and physical health: spending time in the garden is associated with a better sense of well-being. In fact, just 2.5 hours per week spent mucking about in the dirt = better life satisfaction. Known as *therapeutic horticulture*, gardening is a gentle way to get your endorphins up without ruining your knees.

### THE PEP TALK

Luckily for those of us who live in high-rise flats with no garden (and for those of us for whom the word 'hobby' might seem like too much commitment), there are many different ways to 'do' gardening.*

---

*If you can call putting a pot on your windowsill gardening. Which we do.

*Step One*: Decide what you'd like to grow and buy some seeds.

Flowers, herbs, fruits, vegetables or dandelions – the world is your oyster! Pick something you'll enjoy taking care of and then mourn when it eventually dies because gardening is difficult. Easy options for growing indoors include radishes, basil, peppers, tomatoes, marigolds and cosmos.

*Step Two*: Get a lovely pot or two\* that makes you happy to look at and add some fertilised soil from a garden shop.

*Step Three*: Plant your seeds.

Follow the directions on your seed packet – usually you'll want to place them an inch or so deep and a few inches apart. Cover everything up and sprinkle with a bit of water until the soil is wet. Then put the pot in the sun. Keep an eye on its progress and keep the soil moist. In a few weeks or months, you'll have a new tomato and be much happier. Science says so.

---

\*Again, this is the easy and affordable plant pot method. If you're looking to start a proper garden, buy a bigger bag of soil and a proper gardening book.

# Learn to Bartend and Host a Fancy Cocktail Party

'The trouble with jogging is that the ice falls out of your glass.'

**Martin Mull**

The great thing about marathons is that they take place in the spring and summer months, when the weather is usually quite nice. That means *instead* of marathoning you can train to become a skilled bartender and then host a party outside for all your friends.

## THE PEP TALK

While making cocktails can seem intimidating if you're more of a pint of beer or glass of milk type person, it's actually very easy. The secret is that it's very hard to do it wrong. Mixing some booze in a glass and drinking it? You're 99% likely to be successful, even if you didn't char the rosemary correctly or utilise the latest amaro.

*Step One*: Figure out your signature cocktail.

What's your booze preference? Are you into gin or do you prefer whisky? Do you like light and bubbly or a more medicinal, booze-forward vibe? I can advise, for the purposes of your forthcoming soirée, that a lighter option with a lower ABV keeps the party going longer. For a party of one or two, for example, try an Aperol Spritz or a French 75. For a big group, you can't go wrong with a pitcher of Sangria or Pimm's Cup.

*Step Two*: Take a gander at your cupboards and figure out what supplies you might need.

Here's a basic checklist:

- Cocktail shaker
- Large pitcher
- Long wooden spoon for stirring
- Glassware
- Plastic tablecloth (you will spill things)
- Booze of choice

*Step Three*: Pick a party theme and invite your friends.

There's no need to be all Pippa Middleton about it. Pick something fun like summer solstice or the King's birthday or your cat or Wimbledon. Whatever floats your boat. Make yourself a batch of cocktails – and raise a toast to your new life skill. While some people treat their body like a temple, there's arguably nothing more sacred than the feeling of having a lovely pink- or orange-coloured cocktail in the sun with your friends. Call it a health tonic and join the ranks of the fitness-minded.

# Plan Your Funeral

'I intend to live forever, or die trying.'

**Groucho Marx**

Look, if you're squeamish, you can skip this one – but planning your own funeral can actually be pretty empowering. While everyone out there is chasing immortality with protein powders and fancy running shoes and morning gym sessions, there is something to be said for facing our mortality head on and ensuring ourselves a fab final send-off.

## THE PEP TALK

Whenever you finally peace out, know that you'll be very much missed. And know that your loved ones will wish to honour you in the way you would have wanted.* Whether that means a lovely spiritual celebration and/or a knees-up at your local pub, why not plan ahead? You deserve the best death celebration ever. Plus, it's easy. You'll be gone and won't have to actually do anything. What's better than that?

---

*My dad wanted his ashes scattered in three places: with my mum in a cemetery in the US, with his mum and nan under a tree in Manchester and in a lake in Canada. Why not make your final wishes a big, expensive pain in the ass for your loved ones?

*Step One*: Complete your will.

This is the boring business side of death. It's especially important if you've got kids and assets and whatnot. A solicitor can be enlisted to draw one up or just download a simple template online. This is necessary to do before moving on to the fun part.

*Step Two*: Plan your party.

Think about the venue. Church, pub, hall, garden? Think about the music. Do you want sad emo, traditional hymns or drum and bass? Think about any meaningful scriptures, poems or literary passages you'd like read aloud. Think about what flowers you'd like or what cause everyone should donate to. Basically, how do you want to ensure your very last social event on the planet properly honours how great you are? It's okay if it takes some time to figure this out. Then jot your preferences down somewhere and share your wishes with friends and family.

## 26.2 THINGS TO DO INSTEAD OF RUNNING A MARATHON

*Step Three*: Consider why you're waiting to have a big party until after you're gone.

*See the previous entry: plan an epic cocktail party for your friends and think about living life to the fullest right now.*

# Take Up Watercolours

> 'Part of why I like watercolour
> is that mistakes are visible, and
> you can't really repair much.'
>
> **Chris Raschka**

Watercolour painting is one of the most affordable and accessible art forms for beginners.* Whether you took a class or two at school or you've never picked up a brush, learning to paint is a fantastic

---

*Apart from the adult colouring books.

use of your time, and unlike running a marathon, you'll have something to show for it when you're done.

---

### THE PEP TALK

Watercolours are also one of the oldest forms of art, dating back to prehistoric times when our ancestors used water and pigment to create the earliest cave paintings. So if you're self-conscious about your talents . . . take heart. If you can draw a stick figure, squiggle a snake or make some rain droplets like those ancient artists, you're an artist too.

*Step One*: Hit up a craft store or discount emporium of your choice.

Grab a basic set of watercolours (usually the set comes with a brush) and a pad of paper. Specialised watercolour paper tends to be thicker and more textured than the regular stuff, so unless you want soggy, waterlogged pictures, it's a good investment.

*Step Two*: Make some joyful blobs.

Get the brush wet, dab it around in the paints and make some swirls, streaks, washes – whatever you feel like. Layer the colours. Cover a whole page with indiscriminate experiments. Do this until you feel comfortable with the paints. This loosens you up for the next step, should you choose to take it.

*Step Three*: Figure out what you'd like to create.

Watercolours work well for painting landscapes and still lifes. So find a bowl of oranges, a pink hyacinth or a moody vista and get to work. Draw an outline if you'd like and fill it in with colour. Notice the light and the shadows. When you're pleased with it, sign it and hang it in a little frame. You made that.

# Go Fish (Learn a Card Game)

'Each player must accept the cards life deals him or her; but once they are in hand, he or she alone must decide how to play the cards in order to win the game.'

**Voltaire**

Throughout history, cards and card games have been associated with gambling, drinking and general socialising, which is likely why they're still popular today. The first cards are thought to date back to the Tang Dynasty in ninth-century China, when they were printed from woodblocks. The fifty-two-card deck we know today has become one of the world's most iconic designs – instantly recognisable, and full of possibilities.

### THE PEP TALK

Playing card games (aside from being fun) can aid memory, improve cognitive function, teach social skills and relieve stress. Plus, it's an essential skill to have when the power goes out, or you're on a train with poor reception, or you've decided to bond – analogue style – with your partner.

*Step One*: Choose a card game.

There are dozens and dozens of card games one could potentially learn, so pick one that aligns with your goals. Are you looking for a solitary endeavour to pass the time on a long commute? Or do you want something social that can be played in a big group? If it's the former, you'll want to learn Solitaire, of course, and if it's the latter, then poker is a good choice. If you're playing with kids, then Go Fish is your go-to.

*Step Two*: Find a fun deck* that you'll enjoy using.

Decks range from highbrow artistic to lowbrow and naughty, and everything in between. Once you've found one you like, familiarise yourself with the cards. Try shuffling them a bit. Don't be shy.

---

*To truly excel at your new hobby, you're going to need a physical deck. Online games, while convenient, deprive you of the tactile sensation that's a key part of the experience.

*Step Three*: Learn the rules and play the game.

Practice makes perfect and the best way to hone your skills is to play.

# Go Wild Swimming

> 'Live in the sunshine, swim the sea, drink the wild air.'
>
> **Ralph Waldo Emerson**

While the concept of swimming in lakes has been around presumably forever, *wild* swimming is the modern hipster version of that. It usually refers to paddling about in cold water rather than warm, so this activity is best performed somewhere that makes you worry about having a heart attack whilst engaging in it. Scotland, Finland, Quebec, etc.

## THE PEP TALK

Yes, it's very cold. That's the whole point, apparently: doing something that's a bit of a shock to the system, but then very rewarding and brag-worthy afterwards. The benefits are said to be numerous: better circulation, improved sleep, reduced inflammation and boosted muscle strength. Small studies have reported an increase in participants' mental health after eight swim sessions outdoors and improved feelings of well-being after six weeks.

*Step One*: Find yourself a bathing suit.

Also some swim slippers for the rocky shorelines. Find a buddy or swimming group to go with. And find a lake, river or ocean to swim in. Placid is good, with few waves, if any. Check the weather reports (nothing beats a sunny day for outdoor swimming) and head on out.

*Step Two*: Get in the water slowly until you're completely submerged.

Tread water or paddle around for a bit – five minutes is the recommended max for your first time – then head out* and have some tea and cake while wrapped in a warm towel with the car heater running. Enjoy the endorphin rush.

*Step Three*: Repeat for six weeks until those feelings of well-being are manifested.

---

*Remember to always get out of your wet gear immediately or you'll risk hypothermia.

# Adopt a Rescue Animal (Goose or Snake)*

> 'Until one has loved an animal a part of one's soul remains unawakened.'
>
> **Anatole France**

*For wildlife rescues, check local laws and regulations and use your common sense. Having a goose may be fine on your farm in Cornwall. Less so in your Brixton flat. Also, badgers are illegal to have as pets in the UK, thanks to the Badgers Act of 1973 – so you've been warned. No otters, either.

If you can afford the upkeep, including food and vet visits, and you're home frequently enough to provide them with the love and care they need, and you're not allergic, then a pet – a rescue pet – is necessary for living a full and complete life.

### THE PEP TALK

Did you know the mere act of petting an animal can reduce your blood pressure? Pets can also help combat loneliness, improve mental health and even give our lives meaning. Some studies show that pet owners live longer than non-pet owners as a result of all these benefits.

*Step One*: Find your animal.

Finding an animal* that needs a good home is fairly easy. Whether you're a dog person, a cat person or looking to adopt a fish or gerbil for some reason, there's likely a rescue organisation like the RSPCA nearby that can help find you a new best friend. Head on over and meet the animals. If you're lucky, your new family member will choose you – sort of like Paddington Bear and the Browns.

*Step Two*: Prepare yourself.

Prep your home, purchase supplies (you can often find gently used items on offer from other pet owners on local online marketplaces) and find a veterinarian so you can arrange any vaccinations or procedures required for your new family member.

---

*Dogs are the most work, while cats are a bit more self-sufficient. Fish are probably the quietest. Find one that fits your vibe.

## 26.2 THINGS TO DO INSTEAD OF RUNNING A MARATHON

*Step Three*: Prepare to live longer, sleep better and take more photos than you ever thought possible.

# Refurbish an Old Bit of Furniture

It's not a secret that furniture made today is a tiny bit worse than the furniture made in yesteryears. Chipboard, glue and veneer have replaced solid wood, dovetail joints and hand-carved flourishes. On the one hand, lower production costs mean new furniture is more affordable than ever. On the other, it means items won't last as long and are more likely to end up in landfill. That's where your new project comes in: finding and refurbishing something old and lovely.

## THE PEP TALK

Refurbishing can mean many things – and this project can be as easy or as involved as you like. Whether you decide to swap out some knobs on an old dresser, paint a nightstand or sand and stain a big dining-room table, the process of caring for something and giving it pride of place in your home is a nice thing to experience.

*Step One*: Find the furniture.

Finding an item of furniture to restore is the most fun part of the process. Hit up a car boot sale, flea market, your local charity shops, online marketplaces and freecycle groups. Look for items made of solid wood (usually that means they're very heavy or that your gran has the same one) or just pick something that looks like it needs some love. Then find a friend with a work van or pop it in the back of your car or a taxi, and head on home to get started.

*Step Two*: Restore it.

Bring your bit of furniture back to your garage or garden or any place that's well ventilated. Place it on a drop cloth (a fancy word for an old sheet) and decide what type of restoration you'd like to do. The first step is usually to wipe down your new find with a damp rag. Then sand, paint, stain, gloss, oil and buff until it's glorious – remember to wear a mask to protect yourself from dust and fumes. There are loads of videos online that can walk you through this process so if you get stuck, consult the internet. The point is that you're learning and having fun.

*Step Three*: Post it.

You filmed all that, correct? Refurbishing videos are very popular. Post the video and consider whether 'refurbisher' should be your new career. If marathon runners can get applause just for putting one foot in front of the other, you can get some clout for working an electric sander.

# Learn Five Phrases in a New Language

Try resisting the urge to speak in English all the time when you're travelling – even when you're sitting in a British pub, eating a full English, drinking a pint of bitter and watching Man City in Tenerife or the Algarve. Learning just a few words and phrases in the local language is easy, polite and rewarding.

## THE PEP TALK

Apparently, it takes 600 hours to become proficient in a new language. Luckily for all of us, it takes just a few hours to learn a couple of phrases. There are myriad ways of learning these days, including apps, online videos, workbooks, audiobooks and in-person classes. Which is great news because learning languages can improve memory, boost concentration and enhance feelings of empathy. As a bonus, of course, it can help you communicate in a foreign country.

*Step One*: Choose a language.

Pick a language you've always wanted to learn. Or the language that is spoken in your upcoming holiday destination. Then try out a few ways of learning and see what sticks. Do you prefer to see the words and phrases spelled out? Or is learning via audio easier for you?

*Step Two*: Learn some common phrases.

These could be: 'Good morning', 'Please' and 'Thank you', 'Goodbye', 'Cheers', 'Excuse me' and 'Sorry'. Write them down and say them out loud until they stick. Within a few hours you should be able to remember the basics. Then do it again the following day.

*Step Three*: Practise your new phrases when you're on vacation.

If you're uncertain or embarrassed, that's totally normal. Try starting with something small, like 'Thank you'.* Work your way up to 'I'd like two beers, please.' Locals will appreciate the effort, and you'll feel a warm glow at having put yourself out there.

---

*Merci*, *köszönöm*, *danke*, *arigatō*, *grazie*, *shukriya*, etc.

# Explore Some Cookie Recipes

'Cooking and baking is both
physical and mental therapy.'

**Mary Berry**

There's no real reason to bake these days. Just like you could get in a taxi and get to your destination quickly instead of, say, running a marathon, it's quite easy to saunter over to the shops, or put in an order online, and have some ready-made cookies available for your mouth with very little effort. But like many things that are easy to do, doing them that way is not always the most rewarding way to live. Enter: your very own *Great British Bake Off*.

### THE PEP TALK

Cookies (a word derived from the Dutch word *koekje*) are some of the most fun things you can bake – and the easiest. Many recipes have just three ingredients. Take this one for example: peanut butter, granulated sugar and a large egg. Or this one: butter, sugar, flour. This ease of baking means you can start off modestly, develop your skills and work your way up to some fancier things – chocolate hamantaschen perhaps?

*Step One*: Pick a recipe and gather your ingredients.

You'll need an oven, a baking tray, some cooking spray or baking paper, a mixer, a bowl and some utensils. Follow the recipe to the letter.*

*Step Two*: Make your cookies.

---

*Unlike, say, making a stew, baking requires you to measure things properly. The people who say things like, *cooking is more of an art while baking is more of a science*, are correct.

## 26.2 THINGS TO DO INSTEAD OF RUNNING A MARATHON

If you're making peanut butter cookies, here's what you do:

Heat your oven to 180°C or 350°F. Add a cup of smooth peanut butter, ¾ cup of granulated white or brown sugar and a large egg (minus the shell) to a bowl and mix it all together. Then roll the dough into twelve balls and put them on a greased baking sheet. Smush the balls with a fork until they're about ¼ inch (6mm) thick. Then bake them for 10–12 minutes. Let them cool and enjoy! You're basically Mary Berry now.

*Step Three*: Make some more for your friends.

Once you've tried out some recipes and found your groove, it's time to solidify your friendships by gifting cookies everywhere you go. Housewarming? Cookies. Birthday party? Cookies. Add some cellophane and ribbon and a homemade tag and you'll save money on gifts while spreading a bit of joy wherever you go.

# Become an Amateur Astronomer

> 'For my part I know nothing with
> any certainty, but the sight of
> the stars makes me dream.'
>
> **Vincent Van Gogh**

Along with our oceans, space is the last big frontier. It's too vast to contemplate, really, and yet we as a species have relentlessly contemplated it for as long as we've been around. In fact, the world's largest ever telescope (aptly named the Extremely Large Telescope) is being built right now in the mountains of Chile. One of its goals is to search for planets orbiting other stars. Planets just like ours. So while you likely won't have anything *quite* that sophisticated at your disposal, looking at the stars can still be a rewarding pastime.

### THE PEP TALK

One thing to know about amateur astronomer communities is that they're made up of passionate, friendly people who are happy to share their knowledge. If you've ever encountered these sorts in the park, with their telescopes aimed at the sky, rest assured they'll be happy to chat and perhaps give you a peek at the heavens.

*Step One*: Find your 'why'.

Astronomy is a pastime best suited for the naturally curious. So first, figure out what excites you about the skies. Is it the hunt for new comets? Big events like planetary alignments and solar eclipses? Saturn's dope rings? Or maybe you're just into the fact that the astronomy club meets in your local down the street and they seem like a fun bunch. Once you've found your 'why', you can figure out the 'how'.

*Step Two*: Find a telescope.

In order to see the skies, you'll need a telescope. Check out your local library as they may have one available for lending. You can also find one online or join up with your local club and borrow theirs. While it may be tricky to get the hang of at first, there's nothing like the feeling of locking in on your first planet, bringing it into focus and staring at a piece of the universe as it floats gently just a few inches from your retina.

*Step Three*: Research the stars.

Download an astronomy app. It's helpful because, let's be honest, a lot of those stars look the same. It's handy to have a reference for what you're looking at. Especially if you've brought along your kids or some friends and need to impress them with your amateur astronomy knowledge.

# Mend Your Own Clothing

Sewing is an ancient art – our ancestors used to sew animal skins together with bone or horn needles, using sinew for thread. Since the sewing machine was invented, however, sewing by hand has become a bit of a lost art. That makes learning to sew a rewarding way to honour the past while creating something useful.

## THE PEP TALK

Compared to previous generations, the standards for what makes an acceptable 'mend' have loosened considerably. While our grandmothers may have taken great pride in stitching up a jumper so skilfully that the fix was near-invisible, these days it's fine to use chunky threads, colourful patches, and 'good enough' mends to get our clothing through to the next season.

*Step One*: Purchase a basic sewing kit.

You should be able to find one in a local shop. It should come with a few colours of thread, a few different-sized needles and perhaps an adorable little pair of scissors.

*Step Two*: Thread your needle.

This is easier the younger you are. When you're older, this requires more squinting and a contemplation of your own mortality. Nevertheless, once you've done it, pat yourself on the back. Threading a needle is an accomplishment in itself, so if you mend nothing, you've still managed this.

*Step Three*: Get stitching.

Cut your length of thread and tie a knot in the end. Then stitch your bit of clothing together. You can either do a stitch like a little snake – making a long line of stitches, in and out along a seam. Or you can do 'up and over' stitches and sort of spiderweb the cloth together until the hole pulls closed. These aren't the official sewing terminologies so you'll have to investigate that on your own. But regardless of how you manage it, once completed, you'll have learned a new skill, refurbished a beloved item of clothing and saved it from going to landfill.

## Knit Something

'The only difference between an experienced knitter and a new knitter is that the experienced knitter makes bigger mistakes faster. Be bold; there are no terrible consequences in knitting.'

**Stephanie Pearl-McPhee**

The world's oldest-known knitted thing is a pair of socks from Egypt – proving that even the pharaohs appreciated a warm foot.*

### THE PEP TALK

Knitting can be solitary or social, meditative or mindless. It can lower your blood pressure, relieve stress, and reduce feelings of depression. So whether you join a local knitting circle or learn your craft via some online videos, it's a fun, lifelong skill to cultivate.

---

*The historic socks are actually from the eleventh century, long after the pharaohs. But caliphs enjoy warm feet too.

*Step One*: Buy your materials.

Buy yourself some beautiful chunky yarn and some thick needles – the bigger they are, the more painless it will be to learn. Opt for lighter, solid colours in a wool or wool blend, which will make it easier to see your stitches. Next, familiarise yourself with knitting terminology as best you can: skein, purl, ribbing, frogging, etc.

*Step Two*: Learn your stitches.

The simplest stitch to learn is a garter stitch and the easiest item to knit is a dishcloth (although scarves are also a good option for beginners). Follow along with your instructor and don't be afraid to make mistakes. When you complete your first row, take a moment to celebrate. Then keep going.

*Step Three*: Practise.

Repeat until all your friends and family are the happy recipients of your wonderful scarves, tea cosies, jumpers, mittens and hats.

# Become a Beachcomber

Beachcombing is mindfulness in action. The act of walking along the wavy coastline, perusing the sand beneath your feet for sea treasures, is great fun, great exercise and a bit addictive.*

---

*While this activity is also popular with metal detectorists, the spirit of beachcombing is inherently gadget-free.

## THE PEP TALK

Meandering along a bit of beach in search of a treasure given up by the sea can be one of life's most satisfying endeavours. Perhaps you'll find a message in a bottle or something left over from a shipwreck. What more motivation could you possibly need?

*Step One*: Head to a beach.

If you live near the coast, this is easy. If not, you're going to need to sacrifice for your beachcomber training – head to the nearest beach for at *least* a weekend and commit to walking its shores every morning. Sound tough? It will be worth the slog, promise.

*Step Two*: Start combing.

Go at low tide, keep your eyes on the ground, and pick up (then put back)* whatever items strike your fancy. Perhaps you'd like to concentrate on spotting sea glass, clay or ceramic fragments, wave-worn plastics or bits of fishing line. Whatever you choose, remember to leave anything natural – shells, driftwood, pebbles – as you find it. Keep clear of any marine life you may encounter – nesting sea turtles or sleepy sea lions, and obey all local signage.

---

*The beach is not your personal shopping centre. The Coast Protection Act 1949 prohibits the removal of natural items found along the coast.

*Step Three*: Show off your treasures.

Snap some photos of your finds, have a beach picnic, say hello to some gulls and congratulate yourself on a successful day spent beachcombing. And of course, if you do find any pirate treasure, be sure to alert the authorities.

# Embrace the Supernatural

'Everyone who is seriously involved in the pursuit of science becomes convinced that a spirit is manifest in the laws of the Universe, a spirit vastly superior to that of man, and one in the face of which we with our modest powers must feel humble.'

**Albert Einstein**

Believing in the supernatural was a given when we were children. Ghosts, faeries, extraterrestrials, selkies, Santa. Then we all grew up,* and let's admit it: being an adult can be a bit boring. Luckily, there are a lot of things we still can't explain in the world, which means there's lots left to believe in, too.

### THE PEP TALK

Relinquish your hard-earned scepticism and embrace the joy that comes from believing in the unknown. Believing in something has been shown to offer people a bit of comfort in troubling times – it can even help to relieve anxiety.

---

*Which is fantastic, to be fair. I'm glad we've all made it this far. Good for us.

*Step One*: Find your woo.

Do a ghost tour. A UFO lecture. A sound bath. Take a walk around a cemetery. Watch a documentary about Bigfoot or read a book about ESP. Take a trip to the Scottish Highlands and try to spot the Loch Ness Monster. Move a spoon with your mind.* Subscribe to the *Fortean Times*.

*Step Two*: Do your homework.

Once you've awakened your natural, childlike curiosity, really commit to it and learn all you can about your chosen phenomenon. Discover the quirky, serious, studious, surprising and zany subcultures that surround each phenomenon.

*Refer to the 'Learn a Magic Trick' activity.

## 26.2 THINGS TO DO INSTEAD OF RUNNING A MARATHON

*Step Three*: Embrace your new mindset.

Enjoy being more open to the wonderful unknowns of the universe. And then next time something happens that you can't explain – whether you call it coincidence, serendipity, synchronicity, Bigfoot or just weird vibes – enjoy the goosebumps.

# Take Dancing Lessons

> 'Never give a sword to a
> man who can't dance.'
>
> **Confucius**

Dancing is a form of self-expression shared by basically everyone on the planet going back millennia. It's easy to understand why. Being in a room heaving with people, all moving their bodies together, is one of life's greatest, most primal joys. When the music, the crowd and the vibes are just right, dancing can feel transcendent.* (If you're not good at the spontaneous kind, however, you can just take a few classes.)

> ### THE PEP TALK
>
> Dancing helps build muscle tone, improves balance and coordination, and it's a great social activity, too. It's even recommended for people with specific medical issues like Parkinson's. For getting in shape while building connection with your fellow humans, there's no better endeavour.

---

*Sort of like a runner's high, one might imagine. Except with more alcohol and fewer stopwatches.

*Step One*: Decide which kind of dance you'd like to learn.

Salsa is a favourite for beginners – it's upbeat and very social. Line dancing is an excellent choice if you enjoy country music. The waltz is an old-school classic, as is Irish dancing. Many studios and community spaces offer free dance classes or workshops – so try out a couple of styles and figure out what makes you happy.

*Step Two*: Try to attend class at least once a week.

You can practise at home with online tutorials, too. Just remember that dance is best done in person. After a few weeks you should have the basic steps down and be able to put on a little show, should you so desire.

## 26.2 THINGS TO DO INSTEAD OF RUNNING A MARATHON

*Step Three*: Enlist a friend, spouse or crush as your next dance partner.

Invite them to a class or out for an evening of entertainment. Whether you're vogeing in a club or high-stepping in a school gymnasium, dance is an activity that's meant to be shared.

# Write a Poem

'Poetry is a deal of joy and pain and wonder, with a dash of the dictionary.'

**Khalil Gibran**

Poetry is one of the world's oldest and most respected art forms. Before people could read or write, they passed down information from generation to generation in the form of songs or chants. In many countries poets are still held in the highest regard. It's also one of the most accessible forms of creative writing for beginners. Not because it's easy, but because writing something on the shorter side feels less daunting.

## THE PEP TALK

Creative activities like writing poetry are good for your brain, and the rhyming can even help with memory retention. Additionally, writing a good rhyming poem is one of the truest, nerdiest joys in life. Creating a tight scaffolding of your own words that communicates a deep feeling or a story – well, finish this exercise, and you'll see what I mean.

*Step One*: Read some poetry.

Before you fly the plane you must study the manual (one hopes). Luckily, there is poetry for everyone's taste. Start with some classic chaps like Kipling and Wordsworth. Then read some modern icons like T.S. Eliot, Sylvia Plath, Carol Ann Duffy and Jackie Kay. If you enjoy poets exclaiming over vases, you may prefer an ode. If you prefer reading about drugs, the Beat Poets are a good option. Finally, for pure entertainment, you can always pick up a good book of bawdy limericks. The point is to find something you respond to and enjoy – so don't worry if the famous stuff doesn't work for you.

*Step Two*: Decide on style.

Pick the type of poem you'd like to try to write. A haiku can be a good starting point because it offers an easy formula to follow: three lines of five, seven and five syllables each. If that structure feels too constricting, free verse can also be rewarding. There are no rules here. Just write what you feel.

*Step Three*: Perform your poem.

The third and most advanced step in the poetry-writing process is to read your work aloud to someone you trust. Or to a room full of strangers. Whatever makes you cringe less. But part of the essential practice of poetry – or any writing, really – is to share your work. So find an open-mic night or ask your friend or partner to have a listen. And you thought running a marathon was hard! If it helps, here are some terrible limericks to get you inspired:

> There once was a poet from Fife
> Who'd read odes aloud to his wife
> *O Captain, My Captain*
> He'd write on a napkin
> (A plagiarist he was, for life.)

> There was a young chap from Corfu
> Who put all his poems in a stew
> 'The haikus taste the best,'
> he announced. And the rest?
> 'Are flavourless, rather like glue.'

## Make Your Own Jam

> 'My signature jam is damson or quince, and it's called "Kate's Sweet and Sticky". Basically, I'm a domestic goddess.'
>
> **Kate Moss**

Making jam is something we used to do when berries were fresh and in season – before all our jam was made in factories to be consumed year-round. Yes, it's easier to purchase jam from the shops, but making your own is a meditative, cost-saving and useful practice that also happens to be low-impact and safe on your joints (sorry, marathoners).

---

### THE PEP TALK

Our grandmothers did it. So can we.

---

*Step One*: Choose your fruit.

The nice thing about making jam is the plethora of berry options available. Are you a gooseberry girl or do you rate rhubarb? Raspberries are an easy fruit to start with as they mash up nicely and don't have any skins like peaches or plums. Along with a whack of your favourite fruits you'll need some sugar, some half-pint jars and a big pot.

*Step Two*: Get cooking.

Using a ratio of 2:1 fruit to sugar, dump everything into the big pot and mash it around. Bring it to a rolling boil while stirring slowly – and watch out for the jammy overflow. Once the mixture reaches your preferred consistency, spoon the jam into the half-pint jars, seal them and keep them in the fridge.*

---

*This easy jam recipe must be kept in the fridge (or freezer) and is good for a few months. If you're looking for canned jams there are lots of resources that can walk you through that process.

*Step Three*: Enjoy your fresh, homemade jam.

You can serve it on toast, scones, over ice cream or just eat it out of the jar. If you've made too much, give some as gifts. Give your jam a lovely name like Kate Moss did. We're all domestic goddesses now.

# Take a Pottery Course

'The attractions of ceramics lie partly in its contradictions. It is both difficult and easy, with an element beyond our control. It is both extremely fragile and durable.'

**Isamu Noguchi**

Pottery is one of the world's oldest inventions. Archaeologists can determine a wealth of info about a civilisation just from the shards they left behind.* A handmade clay figurine found in the Czech Republic, for example, dates back to around 28,000 BCE, and the earliest known clay vessels date as far back as 18,000 BCE. These days, pottery is both practical and decorative – so make a coffee mug or a dinosaur. Or a dino mug. Whatever you fancy.

### THE PEP TALK

Despite how intimidating this activity might seem at first, the barrier to entry (and to success) is actually quite low. So, if throwing a pot on a traditional potter's wheel – the kind you see in films – is a bit intimidating (or too expensive) then just buy a lump of clay and get to work mashing it about. It's meditative, creative and fun.

---

*If you're worried about your own mortality then pottery is a great skill to learn. Make something that future archaeologists will marvel over. Don't forget to sign your work.

*Step One*: Find a pottery class in your neighbourhood.

Look for a course that includes instruction along with the clay, materials and use of the kiln. If you'd prefer something more self-led, then find one that lets you potter around by yourself.

## 26.2 THINGS TO DO INSTEAD OF RUNNING A MARATHON

*Step Two*: Start with something simple.

The easiest thing to make out of clay is a pinch pot. This is when you take a small ball of clay and smoosh it in the centre with your thumb until it forms a little bowl. Ashtrays are pretty easy, too.*

*Step Three*: Glaze and fire your pottery.

When you have your final piece, you can use it, gift it or put it on a shelf. Then start making something new.

---

*You don't need to take up smoking in lieu of running marathons. However, if you should find yourself in need of an ashtray, it's nice to have one that's handmade.

# Master a Magic Trick

'I am a great admirer of mystery
and magic. Look at this life –
all mystery and magic.'

**Harry Houdini**

Even the world-weary sceptic loves a good magic trick. A rabbit in a hat, a card trick, a disappearing dove – it's nice to be entertained by something we don't quite understand. Everyone should have at least one trick in their repertoire. It makes you more interesting at parties.

### **THE PEP TALK**

Performing magic tricks can be great for your self-confidence and public speaking skills. It can also improve cognitive function and focus. Watching a magic trick has benefits too! One study suggests it can increase creativity in kids.

*Step One*: Find a magic shop.

They still exist in many cities, although they're much rarer than they used to be. The world's oldest family-owned magic shop, Davenports, is in London. Pop in. Have a chat and get some recommendations. Pick up something fun.*

---

*Magic tricks are a very physical, real-world, community-based activity. Going to a shop is a key part of this exercise. If it's cold out or you hate sunlight, you can also do everything online.

*Step Two*: Learn your trick.

Practise your trick at home in front of the mirror or with your friends. Record yourself and watch the video back – the more you practise, the better your trick will be.

*Step Three*: Do your trick out in the real world.

Perform it for a niece or nephew or your co-workers or a grandparent or at a cocktail party. Take satisfaction in offering other human beings a bit of wonder. You're providing a much-needed service in the world.

# Become Known for Sending Handwritten Letters

The mail isn't proper mail anymore, and it hasn't been for ages. Adverts, bills, jury summonses – not exactly inspiring stuff. But those of us who remember the age of postcards, letter-writing and packages understand what's been lost. Luckily, it's easily rectified by this next project. Grab a pen and paper and let's get started.

## THE PEP TALK

The act of physically writing a letter can boost brain activity, improve coordination and enhance feelings of calm.* The act of *receiving* a letter can inspire feelings of goodwill towards its sender (that's you). It's a win-win.

*It's hard to get stressed out when you're holding a really nice pen and writing nice things to someone you care about.

*Step One*: Gather your tools.

To become a first-rate letter-writer, you'll first need the proper kit. Wander out to a gift store or stationery shop and peruse the aisles until you find something that's deserving of your thoughts. Or perhaps you've already got a box of notecards at home you've been meaning to send. Pick up some stickers, stamps, glitter pens or anything else fun that you'd like to use to enhance your missives.

*Step Two*: Choose your recipient and write to them.

It can be a friend who lives overseas or one who lives across town. A beloved niece or nephew. A classmate from uni. A crush. You can write anything, really: a few thoughts, or a stream-of-consciousness confession, or a joke or quote you heard, or paint a little watercolour. Don't worry about spelling errors either (you can cross them out) or about saying everything perfectly. Even a signed postcard with a smiley face on it can be a great way to get started.

*Step Three*: Make a habit of sending physical cards, notes and letters throughout the year.

Whether it's the holidays, a birthday, a thank-you, an anniversary or 'just because', the point is to let people know you're thinking of them. Each handwritten thing you pop in the post will make someone's day brighter.

# Learn to Identify Seven Birds

'I would like to paint the way a bird sings.'

**Claude Monet**

Birding as a leisure activity has been around since the 1700s. The term is preferred over 'birdwatching' because one identifies birds as much by sound as by sight. Whatever you call it, the point of birding is to spend more time in nature.*

---

*It's like golf, but more affordable.

## THE PEP TALK

The UK is a birding paradise. With more than six hundred species – and about thirty that regularly appear in gardens across the country – birds are easy to find. Even easier if you travel to national nature reserves in places like Shetland or the Isle of Wight. Listening to birdsong has a lot of benefits like reducing cortisol levels in the body, improving feelings of calm, tranquillity and well-being.*

*Unless you're listening to crows or gulls. Those are a bit more stressful.

*Step One*: Grab a birding book.

Find one that covers species common in your region and includes excellent photos. The National Trust, the Natural History Museum and the Royal Society for the Protection of Birds all have great online resources, too.

*Step Two*: Familiarise yourself with a couple of species common in your area.

Have a listen to their songs online and then head out (with your book in hand). You'll often hear birds before you see them, so here's a quick guide to the sounds of a few you'll likely encounter:

- Crow (loud caws)
- Robin (early-morning whistles)
- Blackbird (clear, short, clipped chirps)
- Owl (like what you hear in cartoons)
- Great Tit (two chirpy notes that alternate)

*Step Three*: Get a birdfeeder.

There's nothing like the first time a bird alights at your feeder and you realise, with great joy, that it's a tit! Pretty soon you'll own a pair of binoculars and have a favourite bird. Welcome to the world of birding.

## Start a Compost Heap

'The ground's generosity takes in our compost and grows beauty! Try to be more like the ground.'*

**Rumi**

The world's very earliest farmers practised composting, as did the Greeks, Aztecs, Haudenosaunee, Romans and Chinese cultures, among others. Back then, good, healthy crops were a serious business.

---

*A good New Year's resolution if I've ever heard one.

So, we learned from the best and here we are – composting our little bits of earth! Future anthropologists will be impressed with our efforts, surely.

### THE PEP TALK

Compost reduces household waste, promotes healthy plant and flower growth and conserves water. Talk about long-term benefits. If you've got the time and patience to train for a marathon, you'll be well suited to the long-term commitment it takes to compost your food scraps. It's very exciting when you start off, and then quite tedious, and then exciting again. Ready? Set. Go!

*Step One*: Pick a spot for your compost pile.

For beginners, buying or sourcing a purpose-made bin may be preferable as it helps keep everything contained and can keep the critters away. Place it within reach of your garden hose.

*Step Two*: Add some 'browns' and 'greens'.

'Browns' are rich in carbon (leaves, cardboard, sawdust, twigs) and 'greens' are rich in nitrogen (food scraps, coffee grounds, eggshells, teabags, grass clippings). The suggested ratio to aim for is about 4:1 brown to green. Mix every week or two to increase oxygen flow and ensure the compost stays moist.

*Step Three*: Use your new compost.

It can help to fertilise the plants you grew in the very first activity in this book, 'Plant Something'. See? Full circle.

# Write to Your MP

'The best argument against democracy
is a five-minute conversation
with the average voter.'

**Winston Churchill**[*]

The UK Parliament has 650 members. That's a lot of elected representatives just waiting to hear from you – their constituents.

---

[*] Possibly. It certainly sounds like something he could have said.

## THE PEP TALK

Democracy is imperfect, but it works best when we're all involved and paying attention. That's why contacting your MP is an easy, simple way to make your voice heard as often as you like. It's also useful for building a sense of community, fostering feelings of trust and providing a sense of purpose.

*Step One*: Look up your MP on the UK Parliament website.

It's okay if you're not quite sure who they are or how to contact them. Just pop in your postcode, and the site will display your MP's details.

*Step Two*: Figure out what you care about.

The great thing about writing to your MP is that you can write to them about whatever you want, big or small. Perhaps there's a junction in your neighbourhood that needs a pedestrian crossing. Maybe you want to protest against a war or save the penguins. Perhaps you'd like to see more school funding or none at all.

*Step Three*: Take action.

Not getting the results you'd hoped for? Time to run for office. Or volunteer. Or perhaps, just keep writing in. There's no wrong way to do democracy. Except when it all goes sideways, as it's wont to do. Perhaps Churchill was right after all.

# Train for a Long-Distance Walk (Slowly)

'Walking is man's best medicine.'

**Hippocrates**

Unlike running a marathon, going for a walk is an achievable and healthy endeavour that most of the population can undertake without fear of a heart attack or knee injury. And while going to the shops or walking around town is easy enough, planning a walking holiday requires a bit more planning and, yes – even some training.

> ## THE PEP TALK
>
> The UK is full of scenic coastlines, mountains and moorlands made famous by poets, wanderers, novelists and travel programmes. All of them are suitable for long walks with inns, pubs and interesting sights to see along the way. Where there's a will, there's a walk.

*Step One*: Find your route.

Find a scenic route that strikes your fancy and plot out your holiday. Consider joining a tour group if you prefer having your itinerary planned or scour the message boards for insights and forge your own path (one that's likely been trodden for centuries by the Romans, Celts, etc., but still). Decide the total number of days you'd like to walk and how many miles you'd like to aim for per day.

*Step Two*: Get the gear.

If you're a person who likes to gear up, then do so. Get your walking poles, sturdy boots, woollen jumpers and broad-brimmed hats in order. Don't forget your sun cream and insect repellent.

*Step Three*: Practise.

Try out a few day trips first before embarking on the big adventure. The National Trust has some lovely introductory walks on its website – from a couple of miles to 10 miles and more. Ensure that your boots are broken in, you're comfortable walking longer distances and that your walking partner or group won't drive you mad. Then you'll be off to the races!*

---

*Although, of course, you won't be. These are marathon alternatives, remember.

# Learn to Change a Tyre

> 'I may be a living legend, but that sure don't help when I've got to change a flat tyre.'
>
> **Roy Orbison**

If you're a motorist out and about in the world, you will eventually get a flat tyre. The easiest way to remedy this, perhaps, is to call roadside assistance and have someone come and take care of it for you. Ideally, you'll be on the road again in an hour or two. If you're somewhere remote without mobile reception, however, or your phone is dead or you're in a desperate hurry to get where you're going, knowing how to change a tyre is a great skill to have. Think of it as a gift to your future self.

## THE PEP TALK

Despite the best efforts of our tech overlords to mitigate this, we are occasionally required to leave our comfortable virtual environments and deal with analogue, real-world issues. A flat tyre is a perfect example of this, but there's no need for panic. It just takes some strength and a bit of patience – I have faith in you.

*Step One*: Find your spare.

Ensure you've always got a spare tyre in the boot along with a jack and a wheel nut wrench.

*Step Two*: Pull over safely to the side of the road.

Make sure it's a safe place to stop. Take a moment to collect yourself if necessary. Depending on the situation, getting a flat can be a bit of a scary experience. Then get your spare tyre and tools from the boot. Loosen the wheel nuts* with the wrench. These are the big things holding your tyre to your car. Then use the jack to raise up the car frame so the tyre is a few inches off the ground. Twist the wheel nuts off the rest of the way and pull the tyre towards you until it comes off. Hot tip: place the wheel nuts somewhere safe so they don't roll away.

---

*Remember: lefty loosey, righty tighty. In other words, twist anticlockwise to remove.

## 26.2 THINGS TO DO INSTEAD OF RUNNING A MARATHON

*Step Three*: Put the new tyre on.

Lightly tighten the wheel nuts on the new tyre before using the jack to lower the car. Once the car has been lowered, tighten the wheel nuts the rest of the way and you're all set! Don't forget to put the flat tyre, jack and wheel nut wrench back in the boot. Also, give yourself a pat on the back for being so self-sufficient.

# Watch a Marathon

> 'We can't all be heroes because someone has to sit on the kerb and clap as they go by.'
>
> **Will Rogers**

Watching a marathon race offers you all the endorphins that come with running (probably) along with the knowledge you're doing a good deed (you're so supportive!). First, find a map of the marathon route and pick a spot close to your house – a spot that involves the least amount of nonsense and that's preferably close to a toilet. (The only nappies here will be on the marathon runners.) Remember, there will be road closures and lots of 'you can't get there from here' moments.

Bring a folding chair. Pack a lunch. Bring a Thermos of coffee or take some MDMA. Mix a batch of your now-famous cocktails. And clap and cheer the masses as they run along the road for hours at a time, for some reason. Read the funny T-shirts.

Enjoy the various costumes (inflatable dinosaurs, the runaway bride, etc.) and bask in the warm glow that comes from watching people push their bodies to the absolute limit and have fun whilst doing it.

No need to wonder what it feels like. You'll likely never know. And that's just fine. Then head home for a nap. You've done your part and now it's time to rest.

# The Finish Line

> 'I don't believe in jogging. It extends your life, but by about the same amount of time you spend jogging.'
>
> **Marshall Brickman**

Congratulations. You're now a trained expert in 26.2 various activities that have nothing to do with running a marathon. Perhaps you've grown a tomato. Maybe you've won a game of poker with your besties (or confidently lost a few hands at that casino). The world is proud of you. The world is singing your praises. The world values your contributions to society and applauds your dogged pursuit of self-improvement. Too bad they don't give out medals for that sort of thing. You'll have to run a marathon for that. Or, use your new pottery skills and make yourself a celebratory pot. You've earned it.

# Acknowledgements

'Jogging is for people who aren't intelligent enough to watch television.'

**Victoria Wood**

Thank you to my talented editor, Lucy Buxton, for her guidance and patience, and to Lydia Good, for connecting us. Thanks always to my agent, Euan Thorneycroft, at A.M. Heath. Thanks to the whole editorial, design, sales, marketing and PR team at Hodder & Stoughton. Thanks to the booksellers and librarians, and all the readers. And an emphatic 'no thank you' to marathons.

## RAISING READERS
**Books Build Bright Futures**

Dear Reader,

We'd love your attention for one more page to tell you about the crisis in children's reading, and what we can all do.

Studies have shown that reading for fun is the **single biggest predictor of a child's future life chances** – more than family circumstance, parents' educational background or income. It improves academic results, mental health, wealth, communication skills, ambition and happiness.[1]

The number of children reading for fun is in rapid decline. Young people have a lot of competition for their time. In 2024, 1 in 10 children and young people in the UK aged 5 to 18 did not own a single book at home.[2]

Hachette works extensively with schools, libraries and literacy charities, but here are some ways we can all raise more readers:

- Reading to children for just 10 minutes a day makes a difference
- Don't give up if children aren't regular readers – there will be books for them!
- Visit bookshops and libraries to get recommendations
- Encourage them to listen to audiobooks
- Support school libraries
- Give books as gifts

There's a lot more information about how to encourage children to read on our website: **www.RaisingReaders.co.uk**

Thank you for reading.

---

[1] OECD, '21st-Century Readers: Developing Literacy Skills in a Digital World', 2021, https://www.oecd.org/en/publications/21st-century-readers_a83d84cb-en.html

[2] National Literacy Trust, 'Book Ownership in 2024', November 2024, https://literacytrust.org.uk/research-services/research-reports/book-ownership-in-2024

It's Okay to not be Okay

Andrea Guasch

---

It's Okay to not be Okay

Vanguard Press

**VANGUARD PAPERBACK**

© Copyright 2024
**Andrea Guasch**

The right of Andrea Guasch to be identified as author of
this work has been asserted by her in accordance with the
Copyright, Designs and Patents Act 1988.

**All Rights Reserved**

No reproduction, copy or transmission of this publication
may be made without written permission.
No paragraph of this publication may be reproduced,
copied or transmitted save with the written permission of the
publisher, or in accordance with the provisions
of the Copyright Act 1956 (as amended).

Any person who commits any unauthorised act in relation to
this publication may be liable to criminal
prosecution and civil claims for damages.

A CIP catalogue record for this title is
available from the British Library.

ISBN 978 1 83794 134 6

*Vanguard Press is an imprint of
Pegasus Elliot Mackenzie Publishers Ltd.*
www.pegasuspublishers.com

First Published in 2024

**Vanguard Press
Sheraton House  Castle Park
Cambridge  England**

Printed & Bound in Great Britain

To those who are lost and feel alone.

Exhausted

The reason why I keep my feelings to myself
Is because I can't explain them.
I just don't feel anything.

I'm tired of being lost.

I'm tired of having to put on a mask, I'm tired of feeling this way,
I'm tired of not being able to tell anyone how I feel, I'm tired of feeling fat all the time, and
I'm tired of lying.

I haven't felt beautiful in months.
That's the truth.

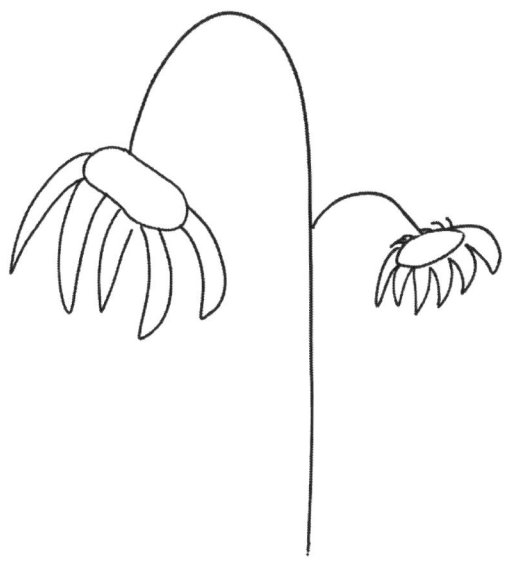

Why am I fat?

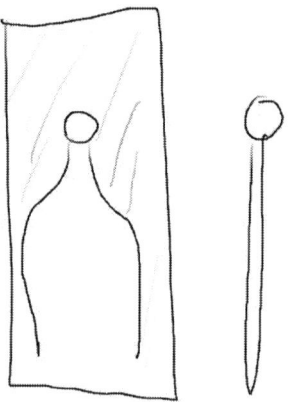

I won't eat! I'll continue doing this.
It hurts, but it's worth it.

Now I understand the pain,
and it's not that bad.

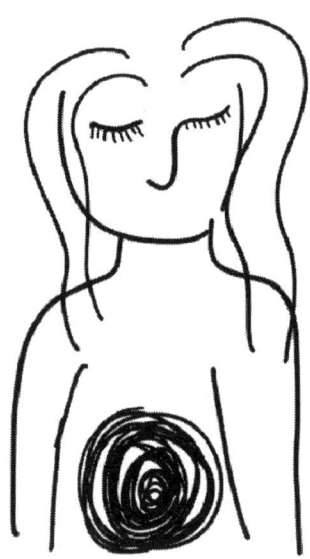

I wish I could grab scissors and cut all my fat.

I'm getting stronger every day.
(In a bad way.)

I just want to tear my skin apart and disappear.

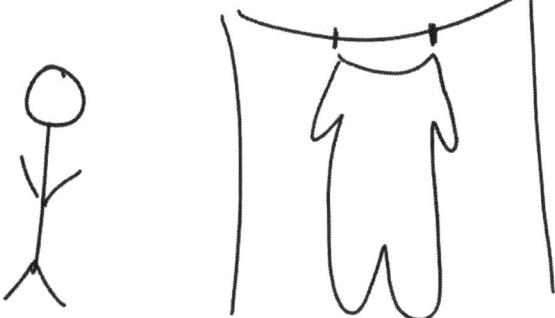

Depression speaks by
letting off tears.

I can't sleep, because my stupid head won't stop thinking about being skinnier…

My fingers are covered in blood.
I hate you, anxiety.

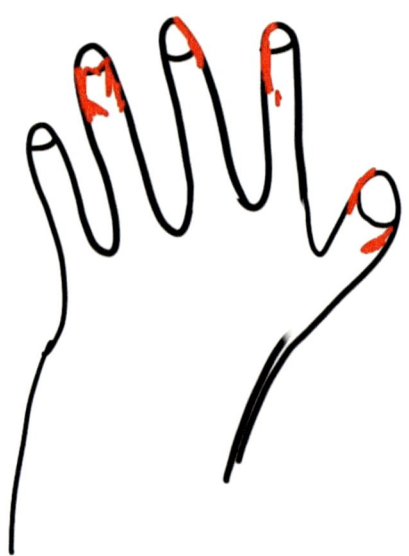

I'm getting used to shaking.

I'm tired of pretending to be someone that I'm not.

I don't know if I'm pretty… I don't know.
I'm crying right now, and I don't even know why.
I need help, but I think people will think that it's just a silly teenage thing…

It's late, and I'm still awake, thinking about how I feel.
I make people believe that I'm happy and that I don't have problems, but that's not true.
I feel like…
I don't know how I feel – that's the worst.
I'm so pressured to get good grades and be perfect, but I don't have any motivation to continue. I can't keep going.
This is too much. I'm in pain, and I don't even know why.
I don't want to be another problem in my mom's life.

"Teenage thing."

Why are my boobs so big?

I deserve this pain.
I have it all under control.
Nobody would understand.
The pain will disappear if I continue.

Looking in the mirror feels like seeing a stranger.

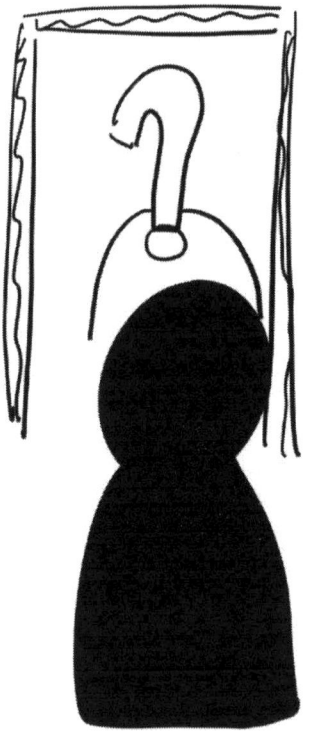

Words that hurt: (Select the ones you have heard too.)

- ☐ It's all your fault.
- ☐ When you try to do something, you make it worse.
- ☐ You're always mad at me, and I don't even know why.
- ☐ Can you be happy for once?
- ☐ Your mood is annoying.

Watching the waves  on the beach
and feeling that I want to swim
and let them make me disappear.

Twelve p.m., and I'm crying again.

I feel so lonely.

I can't look into the mirror without thinking, *Ew.*

I feel so numb today.

AAAAAAHHHHHHHH.

Why is my body so big?

When I show the real me,
people start to get mad at me,
so let's put on the mask again.

I feel so worthless tonight,
I'm such a burden on everyone's life.

I have no place in the world

- I can't stop thinking about jumping into the street. What would happen? Nothing, because nobody cares about me.
- I know I need help, but if I tell my mom, I'm sure she will say it's a teenage thing. She will say that she has lots of problems right now. Also, I don't want to be another one.

(Lies 'the voice' tells me – again.)

I'm scared.
If I do it, it all ends.
No more life.

I hate that stupid voice.
*Shut up!*

I woke up this morning, and I didn't want to get up.
I'm so, so tired.

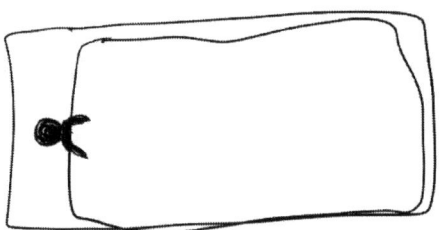

Crying in front of your reflection because you don't know who you are.
(Worst feeling.)

I'm tired of:
>Pretending I'm okay when I'm not.
>Having to be perfect all the time.
>Believing that it will never be okay.
>Thinking that the way I feel is my fault.
>Crying in front of the mirror.
>Feeling fat all the time.
>Feeling alone.
>Putting on a mask every time I want to cry in public.
>Buying clothes that are not for me, or that I don't feel comfortable with.
>Lying to everyone.
>Vomiting.
>Anxiety at night.
>I'm tired of my life; a life that is full of sadness all the time; a life that is full of pain, lies and tears.

I feel nothing, so I make myself feel something.

When I start eating, I can't stop.
I'm hungry all the time.

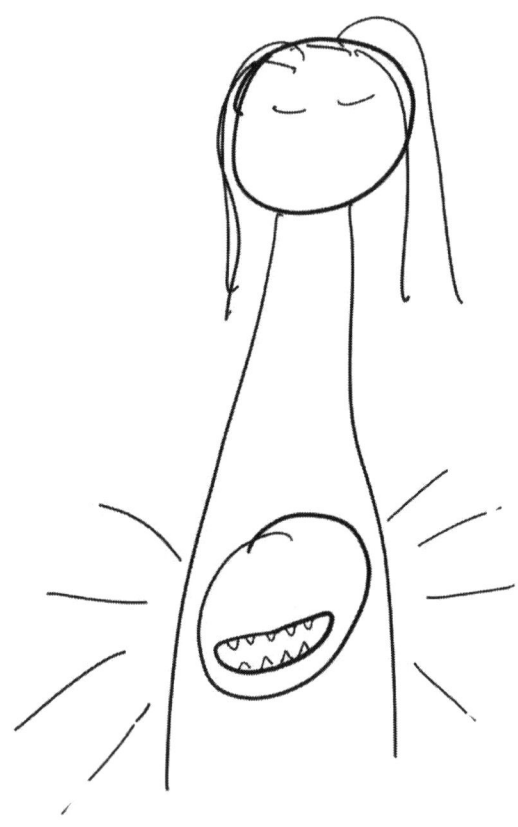

I feel like I'm a visitor in my own mind.

I feel disgusting.

I'm always around people. I always need distractions because
I'm scared of myself – of what I would do, of what she could say to me if I'm alone.

(Stupid voice.)

I feel as fat as the moon when it is full.

When did everything get so hard?
Why is it so hard to stay alive?

Nobody would understand what this feels like –*not feeling anything at all.*

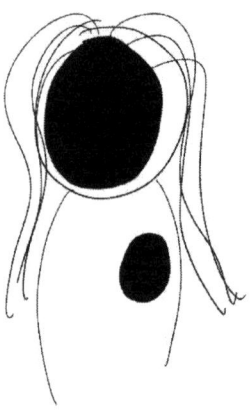

I feel like I hate everyone. I don't know why.
Maybe it's because I see all those happy people, living their happy lives, surrounded by happy people.

The worst feeling is washing your mouth after vomiting.

I'm laying down on my bed, waiting for this day to end, with a hole inside of me that I just don't know how to fill.

Why don't I want to do the things that I like?
Do I still like them?

Enjoy the emptiness of this page.

I was on the front seat of my mobile home, and I was looking through the window when I realised that life is too beautiful to end but too hard to keep going. I took my belt off and went to the bathroom. I locked the door, and I started crying. I looked at myself in the mirror, and I saw nothing. I grabbed the pills that were there and looked at them, thinking, *I want to do this, I want to do this,* while my tears were falling over my cheeks.

All those times I pushed myself to vomit came to my mind. All those nights came to my mind.

I grabbed them, and I put them in my mouth. I was going to do it when something stopped me. The real me came out, the happy one, the one that fights for what she wants, the one that loves laughing, the one that cares about people, the one that loves dancing while it's raining, the one that doesn't give up easily. The real me.

She stopped me and said, "What are you doing? I know that you're struggling and that this is too much for you, but you have to be strong *ask for help,* because you deserve a happy life.

She disappeared with those words. I put the pills where I had found them, I sat down on the toilet, and I looked in the mirror. This time I saw someone – someone that was lost, someone that was sad, someone that needed help. I stopped crying, and I went out of that bathroom, with my head up and with my heart broken.

Summer 2019

ROLLERCOASTER

I'm afraid people are gonna leave me,
because dealing with me and my sadness is too much.

Everything is going so fast.
My mind needs a break.

Wearing baggy clothes is like wearing an armour from the 17$^{th}$ century.
I feel so safe when I wear hoodie and sweatpants.

How am I going to show my body if I don't even like it?

Are you okay?
How are you feeling?
What's going with you?
(Worsts questions.)

Am I a stranger? Why are my friends treating me different? I'm still me…

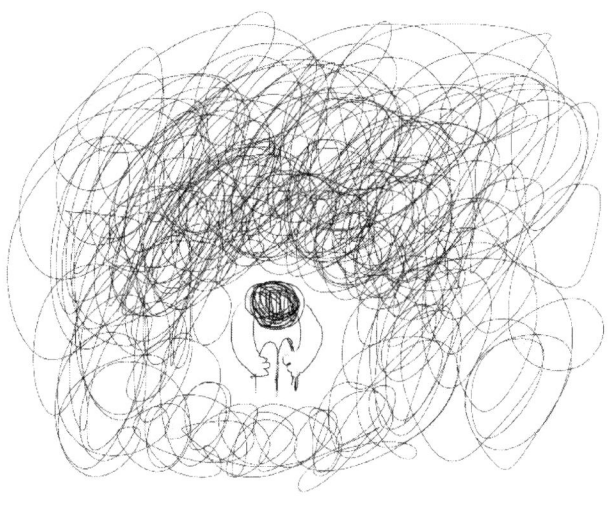

Eating feels so good that it makes me cry.
Eating feels so good that it makes me angry.

I do deserve to eat – everyone does.
But I don't want to be fat.

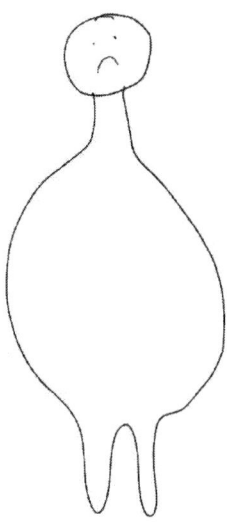

Is it worth it?
All the pain?

Mom and Dad keep shouting at each other on the phone.

I'm just like a cup.
I keep all this water inside until it comes out.

(Crying all the time.)

"I like you better when you are happy."
    Do I look like I care?

I need to be in control of my body and my mind,
and when I eat, I'm not.

I always ruin everything with my sadness.

Sometimes going back to your past is scary,
because you're afraid of getting worse again.

Pain is always there – you have to learn to live with it.

I don't have any control of my life right now, and that makes me feel anxious. My body is shaking. I can't breathe well. I can't speak. I can't walk. I have no control of anything. I keep gaining weight. I need to study for tomorrow's exam; I need to pack my bag and go to my dad's house. I keep biting my fingers. I need to excel in all my exams. I can't breathe, it's happening again. I think it's getting worse. Am I going to die? I think I'm going to faint. I can't even walk or open the door to go ask for help. My vision is blurring.

> Lots of thoughts are coming at the same time, and I can't even concentrate on one thing at a time.

(Panic attack.)

I need to stop surviving and start living, by facing the voice inside of my head.

I need to scream today.

I feel so lonely.
I feel like if I talk too much about my feelings to my friends, they will get tired of me.
I feel like they don't understand me one hundred percent.

Don't wait for someone to get you out of the well. Nobody is going to do that for you, so *do it yourself.*

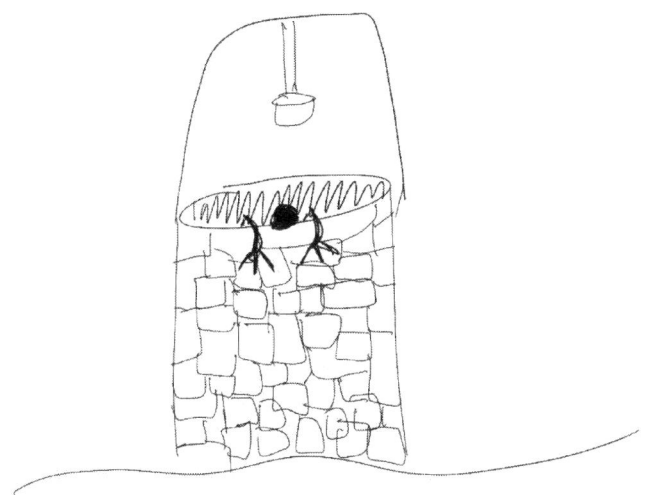

I feel like I need to vomit, but is that really a need or just my head ignoring the fact that I'm getting better?

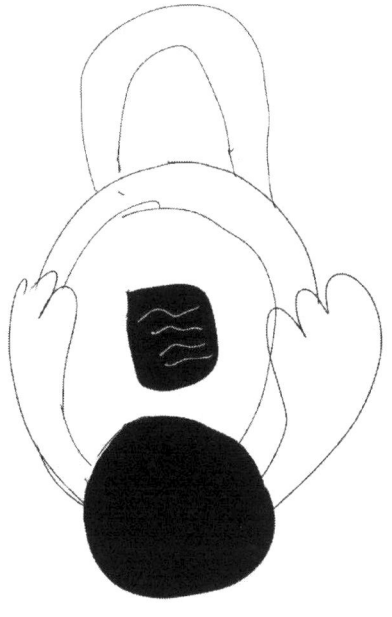

I hate the internet.
All those fake people showing fake lives and fake bodies.

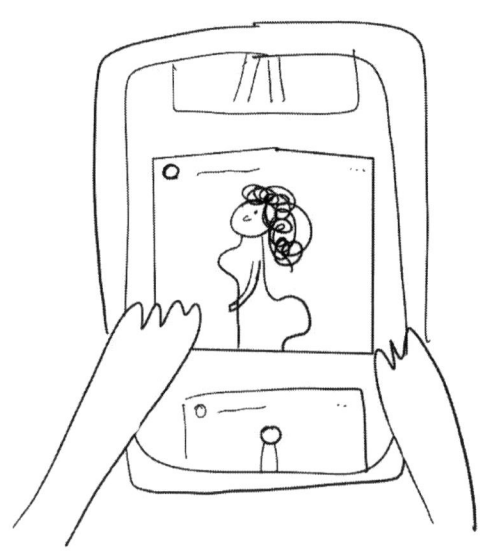

I hate being on a rollercoaster.
Today I feel awful, and yesterday I felt so happy that I wanted to dance all the time.

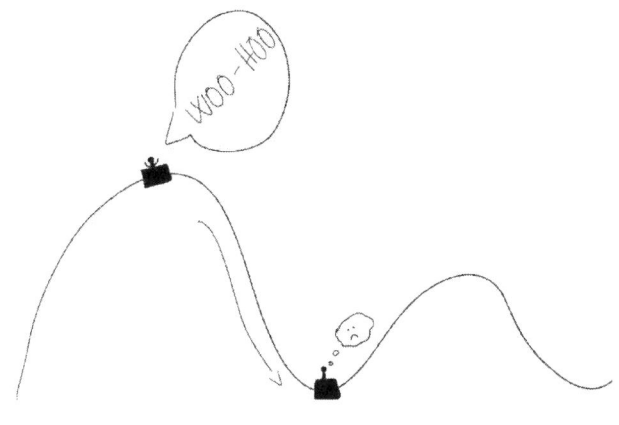

My sadness took care of me – it invaded me in one second.

I want to cry, I want to shout, and I don't even know why.

Now I know that crying doesn't make you an 'emotional' or 'fragile' person.
At some point, we all need to let go of things by letting off tears.
That doesn't make us emotional.
That makes us human.

It's still very difficult to eat.
I always have the fear of going back.

# RELAPSES ARE OKAY

I feel horrible today.
Why did I feel gorgeous yesterday?

So, does it really matter?
Do other people's opinions matter?
Does not being perfect matter?
Does not getting good grades at school matter?
Does not being skinny matter?

My head keeps anticipating everything.
It's so exhausting.
Why can't I enjoy *the moment?*

Why can't I one hundred percent enjoy food?
I just want to eat and not have regrets about it.

We've all got this power, and we don't even realise it.

Pain makes us stronger.
Pain makes us stronger.
Pain makes us stronger.
Pain makes us stronger.
Pain makes us stronger.
Pain makes us stronger.
Pain makes us stronger.
Pain makes us stronger.
Pain makes us stronger.

The hardest thing is to get up in the morning.
I'm all a mess.

I feel so vulnerable when I cry.

*Aaaaahhhhhhhhhh;* I *hate* intrusive thoughts.

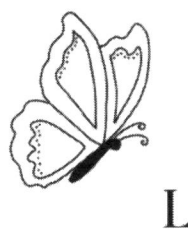
# Light

The truth is that life is very beautiful.
Birds singing in the morning. The sound and the smell of the rain. Long night walks. Laughing until you pee yourself. Dancing under the rain. A hug from a long-distance friend. Drinking water after a walk. The smell of the mountain. Running because it's raining so much. Trying on that new dress. Christmas morning. Studying and actually getting a good grade. Sleeping with Momma.

We don't know what's going on in everyone's life, so don't judge someone by their mood.

Today I feel like saying 'I love you' to everyone.

I still hate most of the parts of my body, but I try to focus on the ones that I love.
Try it, too! Paint those that you love!

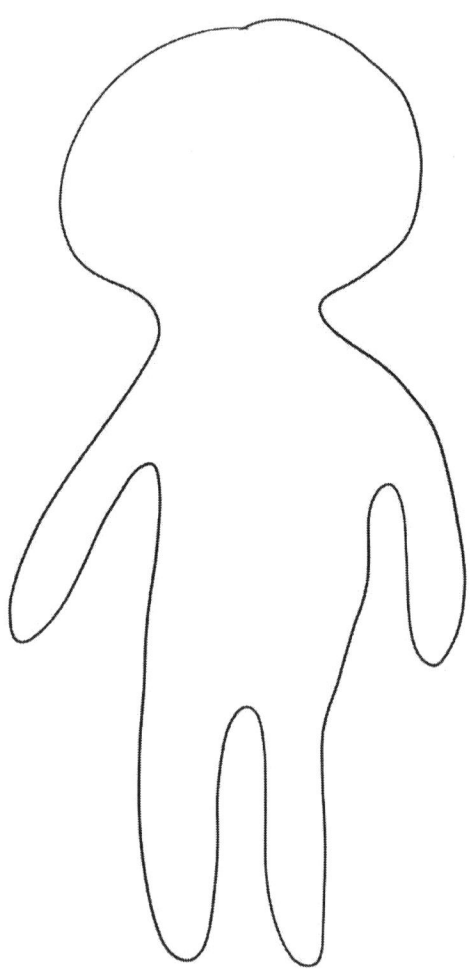

We are *not* the choices we make.

I made some decisions that didn't define me as a human being. My mind made me do some of them, such as pushing myself to vomit or trying to kill myself several times.

I *wasn't* those decisions. They don't define me, and I don't *let* them define me.

What defines us is the strength we have to stand up.

Now I know that without all my past and all the things I've done, I would have never been where I am right now: Loving myself.

Don't be ashamed of your past or of all those things you did wrong, because if you try to learn from them, you will become the best version of yourself.

Trauma doesn't go away, ever. We think it does, but it doesn't.
We have to learn to live with it.
We have to know that if something reminds us of our trauma, we are going to cry.
And that's okay.
So don't be scared of facing it, because you can decide if it can hurt you or not.
You have that power – use it!

We need to take a break sometimes. Studies, work… They take our time and make us tired and sleepy. All we want to do after we finish our labours is sleep. We all need time for ourselves.

So just go for a walk with a friend, sing along to your favourite songs, try to cook something, or go to the forest and paint trees. All those little, tiny things will make a huge difference in your life.

Don't try to impress people – do the things for yourself. People don't really care about other people's success.

Society expects us to not have bad days, days when you need to cry, days when you just need to let go of work or high school.

People think that depression can be turned off, that it's just a "phase" or "moments".
Fuck that!

Try to find the beauty in the small things.

We have to be brave to let go.

We are sad because we keep kept by memories.

We need to love ourselves more when we are a total mess.

If you can't look into any mirror without thinking 'ew',
    just cover all of them.
It's that easy.

(That really helped me.)

Even though we don't see light on our darkest days, it doesn't mean we will be inside the well forever.

There will be days when we won't see progress in ourselves.
Those days we will think that all we have done is useless, so be prepared to fight your voice, because it won't be easy.
We all survive that, and that makes us really powerful.

We can't forget our past, because it makes us who we are.
Without it we wouldn't be where we are.
We can put it back, but never forget where we started.

Pain does not last forever.
        Pain does not last forever.
    Pain does not last forever.
        Pain does not last forever.
Pain does not last forever.
        Pain does not last forever.
    Pain does not last forever.
        Pain does not last forever.
Pain does not last forever.
        Pain does not last forever.
    Pain does not last forever.

We need happy little moments in our life to keep going.

What does your voice say to make you feel worthless?

_____

Now say it with me: "Fuck that; I'm capable of anything!"

It all feels like a spiral when intrusive thoughts come in…

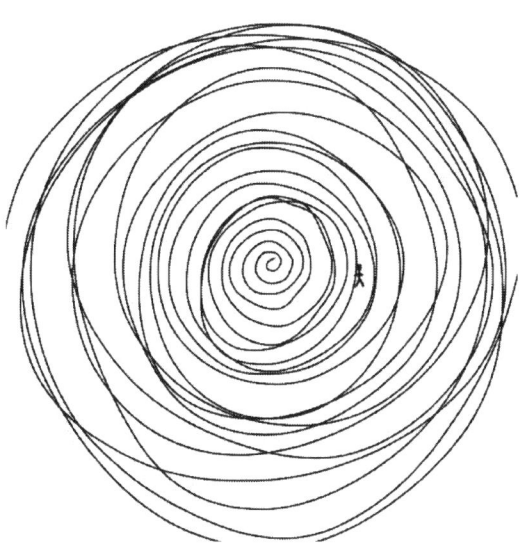

We don't have to be perfect to be beautiful.

CRY IT ALL OUT.

Maybe it's not who we are; maybe it's who we want to be.
We try so hard to change ourselves just to be perfect or accepted.
The problem is the person we want to be or become by getting skinnier.
We can't live with what we have – our own (body. We just need more and more. We even sacrifice our own happiness to be that person.
We even think that we will be happy being skinnier.

*live
right here
right now*

You will be happy – trust me.

Start by getting out of your bed.
Get out of your room and leave your phone there.
Go to the bathroom and face the mirror.
Ask yourself:
- Do I know this person?
- Are you lost?
- Do you need help?
- Are the things that I'm doing normal?

TAKE ACTION OR STAY LIKE THIS FOREVER!

"Nothing changes if nothing changes."
- Albert Einstein

It's okay to make mistakes.
It's okay to relapse.
It's okay that your growth is not straight.
It's okay that, sometimes to be better, we have to go back
   and then forward again.

We need to ask for help when we are feeling down.

I ask my mom for help all the time. She hugs me and tells me that everything is going to be okay.

Asking for help doesn't mean we are fragile, we just need someone to tell us that everything will be okay, because sometimes the stupid voice speaks louder than our head and makes us believe we won't.

ogress I love ss I love my
progress I love my gress I love my p
progress I love my p ogress I love my p
progress I love my progress I love my p
progress I love my progress I love my
progress I love my progress I love m
rogress I love my progress I love
ogress I love my progress I lo
ress I love my progress I
ss I love my progress I
I love my progres
ove my prog
my pr

Don't avoid painful memories.
Don't hide them in the past.
Face them or they will face you.

- The thing is that 'that' voice never disappears. It never goes away.
- You have to learn to live with it. You can turn it down but never mute it.

- When you do something great or look in the mirror and like yourself, you always have that voice that tells you that it's not enough or that you look disgusting.
- We all have to learn to say out loud, "*No,* I won't give you that power. I look awesome and that's it."

I was all broken.
Now I'm starting to get all those pieces together and start building a new me.

I've got scars that nobody sees;
memories that will be forever on my mind
and nightmares that won't ever go away.

**It's okay not to be okay.**
Look at me; of something that wasn't okay I built and found my true self.
So **it's okay** to make bad decisions, **it's okay** to make mistakes, because if you choose to stand up, **the outcome will always be positive.**